GRAIGUENAMANAGH

LEABHARLANN CHO. CHILL CHAINNAIGH

Kilkenny County Library

The Anti-Bully Machine

PAUL SHIPTON

WITHDRAWN

Illustrated by Andy Hammond

OXFORD

UNIVERSITY PRESS

D0270634

Oxford University Press, Great Clarendon Street, Oxford OX2 6DP

Oxford   New York
Athens   Auckland   Bangkok   Bogotá   Buenos Aires   Calcutta
Cape Town   Chennai   Dar es Salaam   Delhi   Florence
Hong Kong   Istanbul   Karachi   Kuala Lumpur   Madrid
Melbourne   Mexico City   Mumbai   Nairobi   Paris   São Paulo
Singapore   Taipei   Tokyo   Toronto   Warsaw

and associated companies in *Berlin   Ibadan*

Oxford is a registered trade mark of Oxford University Press

© Paul Shipton 1999

First published 1999

ISBN 0 19 918700 2

All rights reserved. No part of this publication may be reproduced,
stored in a retrieval system, or transmitted, in any form or by any
means, without the prior permission in writing of Oxford University
Press. Within the UK, exceptions are allowed in respect of any fair
dealing for the purpose of research or private study, or criticism or
review, as permitted under the Copyright, Designs and Patents Act
1988 or in the case of reprographic reproduction in accordance with
the terms of licences issued by the Copyright Licensing Agency.
Enquiries concerning reproduction outside those terms and in
other countries should be sent to the Rights Department,
Oxford University Press, at the address above.

Printed in Great Britain

Illustrations by Andy Hammond

KILKENNY COUNTY
LIBRARY
Acc. No. KK124919
Class No. REM
Inv. No. 15883
Cat. 3 - 5 - 2000

Denis Cartney
£2.25

1

A big secret

KILKENNY COUNTY LIBRARY

We were on a path near the secondary school when some older kids came up behind us. Before we knew it, one of them pulled the bag from my friend Chris's shoulder.

'What's in here then?'

'Give that back ...' began Chris, but the older kid was already unzipping the backpack. He pulled out a coke and a bag of crisps.

3

'Plain crisps? Don't you know I like cheese and onion?'

He tossed the bag to one of his giggling friends.

Chris grabbed for it, but it sailed high over his head. The girl who had the bag now threw it to another kid. She was careful to keep it out of Chris's reach, but she forgot about me. I jumped and caught the bag with one hand.

The kid who'd grabbed the bag in the first place examined me as if I was a new kind of insect. 'Give it here,' he demanded.

'It's not yours,' I said, sounding calmer than I felt.

The big kid smirked. 'Can you prove it isn't my bag?'

'Yes,' said one of his friends, a tall girl with spiky hair. 'I've always liked that bag of yours, Kev.'

Thorny Wood Secondary was just across the way from us. The school was closed – it was still the summer holidays – but a caretaker was working outside the main entrance.

'You all go to Thorny Wood, don't you?' I said. My sister was at the school and the spiky-haired girl was in her class. 'Let's go and ask the caretaker. He'll be able to sort this all out.'

The older kids didn't say anything. They were wondering if I really meant it. They decided I did.

'Come on,' said the other boy. 'Let's go.'

They wandered off in search of different trouble. 'Bye, kiddies,' Kev shouted over his shoulder.

I handed Chris his bag.

'Thanks, Steve,' he said. But he still seemed worried. He was looking at Thorny Wood Secondary. In one week's time we would be starting at Thorny Wood ourselves. Its windows winked at us in the sunshine. At last, Chris asked, 'Do you think there are lots of kids like that there?'

'Don't worry. My sister loves it there!'

THORNY WOOD
SECONDARY
SCHOOL

My older sister Sonya thought the school was brilliant.

Chris nodded but he didn't look as if he really believed me. I knew what he was thinking. We were going to start at a huge new school full of bigger kids and older kids. Would there be bullies everywhere?

I thought for a moment. 'Chris,' I said at last. 'I'm going to tell you a secret. You probably won't believe it, but it's true. It happened at the start of last school year.'

'When you first came here?'

I nodded. 'My family had moved from another town. At the beginning of my final year in the juniors, I was a new kid in the school.'

I took a deep breath.

2

Bully for you

It wasn't too bad being a new kid at first. I liked my teacher, and the kids were really nice. Well, most of the kids were. But there was a problem ...

Meatball Newton and his gang. His real name was Michael, but everyone called him Meatball.

He looked like a gorilla that's been shaved and dressed in a T-shirt, that's what. Like a pro wrestler who'd been sent back to junior school.

Well, OK, maybe not quite so bad, but he was the biggest kid in the school and he knew it. What's worse, he was a bully. And even worse still, he had decided to have some fun with me.

It was a Friday morning. We'd been studying electricity that week, and for my project I'd made a model lighthouse. It had a little lightbulb that flashed on and off when you hit a paperclip switch. It had taken me ages to make and I was pretty proud of it.

So when I saw Meatball and his mates in the playground, I tried to become invisible. No use.

They spotted me and zoomed over like sharks on their way to a fish supper.

KK124919

'Well, well. If it isn't little Stevie.'

I hated that. Just because I'm small! You'd think someone with a name as daft as 'Meatball' would know better than to call names!

Meatball's eye fell on the model lighthouse. 'Hey! What's this?'

He snatched the lighthouse and began clicking the switch on and off. He did it faster and faster until the switch fell apart in his beefy hands.

Meatball beamed. 'Oops! It's bust.'

His two mates, Adam and Phil, sniggered, nodding their heads like those toy dogs in the backs of cars.

'Can't have been much good in the first place, eh?' said Phil.

Meatball tossed the lighthouse model back to me. 'Here yer go,' he sneered.

That meant they were done with me. They stalked off and started booting a football around – someone else's football, of course.

I looked over at the teacher on playground duty. Mr Mullins, the music teacher, was staring into space and humming. He hadn't seen a thing. Now what could I do?

I looked glumly at my ruined model.

Suddenly a kid I didn't recognize was squatting next to me. He was tall and bony. His skinny arms reached out for the lighthouse. 'What are you doing?' I asked.

The boy didn't look up from under the fringe of wild hair that flopped over his forehead.

'Fixing this,' he murmured. He pulled a tiny screwdriver from his pocket.

And that's how I met Neil Gregory.

3

Recognizing genius

The boy's slender hands were a blur.
I just watched in amazement. Every so
often he'd pull some new bit of wire
from his pocket. It took less than a
minute.

When he was done, my model no
longer had a crummy paperclip-switch.
Now it had a proper button set on a
little black box.

'What happens when I press it?'
I asked.

The skinny boy gave an odd little
smile. I pressed the button. The model's
lightbulb began flashing on and off
automatically. It still ran from the same
little battery, but it was much brighter
now.

Then the model let out a noise –
exactly like a foghorn on a real
lighthouse!

'That's incredible!' I said, astonished.

The boy shrugged and stood up.

That's when I realized how tall he was – taller even than Meatball Newton, though he was also much skinnier than the stocky bully. He was the kind of kid who would spend his life being called names like Beanpole, and Lollystick.

I looked up into his face and grinned. 'Bet you get nose bleeds up there ...'

'What do you mean?' The boy stared down at me with pale blue eyes.

I tried to explain. 'You know, because you're so tall ...'

The boy shook his head. 'Ah, well, of course, the difference in atmospheric pressure is practically nothing and so ...'

'It was a joke!' I cut in. The boy blinked a couple of times. He was processing the information. Then he threw back his head and let out a high-pitched giggle.

He sounded more like someone trying to laugh rather than someone really laughing.

'I'm Steven,' I said. 'What's your name?'

'Neil Gregory. I'm a genius.'

I don't know about you, but that struck me as an odd way to introduce himself. *Hello. My name is Neil. I'm a genius.*

'Are you new here?' I asked.

Neil nodded. 'Today is my first day.'

That must be difficult, I thought. At least I had arrived for the start of the school year.

I pointed to the model. 'How did you do that?' I asked.

Neil gave me a big-eyed stare. 'That was nothing,' he said. 'Kid's stuff! Didn't I tell you I'm a genius?'

There he was again with that 'genius' stuff. To be honest, it was getting on my nerves a bit, even if he *had* fixed my model. His gaze didn't leave me. He was starting to make me uneasy.

'Listen,' he said. 'You could come round to my house over the weekend. I'll show you how to do it. It's so easy I could teach a monkey how to do it.'

I hesitated. I hadn't made many friends yet at school, but was Neil the sort of friend I wanted? Something told me that he wouldn't want to boot a football around, or go into town and listen to the new chart songs at the CD shop, or do anything I was interested in.

'Thanks, but I'm ... er ... busy this weekend.' I picked up the model and started to move away.

'Wait!' Neil was digging around in his pocket. 'Let me show you something I've been working on.'

He pulled out a little machine, the size of a tennis ball. A jumble of wires covered it.

I stopped. 'What does it do?'

Neil clicked a button at the base. The machine whirred and began to spin. It went faster and faster until it was just a blur. I was just about to say, 'That's nice!' or something, when it began to float upward.

Honestly! It rose into the air and
hovered just above the ground.

KILKENNY
COUNTY
LIBRARY

I couldn't believe it! I held my breath
in wonder.

'Is it magic?' I asked.

Neil's eyes glittered. 'Better than that. It's electrical engineering. It's *science!'*

Whump! Suddenly a football smashed right into the little floating machine.

There was a cracking sound and then the tinkle of metal and plastic hitting the floor. When the ball rolled away, Neil's machine was smashed beyond repair.

I looked up. Meatball was holding his arms triumphantly above his head.

He had done it on purpose, I knew.

'Who's that?' Neil asked me.

'Meatball Newton. He's a headcase. Stay away from him, if you can.'

But Neil was watching the bully coldly. His blue eyes had turned steel grey. 'Some people should be taught a lesson,' he said flatly.

'Yes,' I agreed. I looked at the tall, skinny, new boy and thought to myself, *But I don't think you're the person to do it.*

'And I know how,' said Neil, darkly.

I don't know why, but a shudder ran down my spine.

4

It's all about attitude

I slept terribly that night. Every time I nodded off, Meatball terrorized my dreams. Only, now, he was a giant who chased me along the school corridors with his enormous head bumping against the ceiling. I tried to escape, but I was powerless to move.

Finally I gave up trying to sleep. I just lay in bed and wondered what to do.

How about karate? If I learnt karate, then the next time Meatball tried anything, I'd demonstrate my lethal karate chop which could smash through the thickest plank. *Haiii-yah!*

Then I'd casually say, 'Just think what that would do to someone's head.'

It was a nice thought, but it wasn't much help. It took years to get good at karate. I needed something fast. I needed to be exposed to a cosmic ray from space or something! You know, like those super-heroes in comics? Then I could fly to school and use my super-strength to deal with Meatball!

OK, face facts, I told myself. *There isn't much chance that you'll gain super powers before Monday morning.*

These thoughts buzzed round and round inside my skull. They were still going strong by the middle of the morning, when my sister Sonya threw a cushion at my head – her usual way of getting my attention.

'Come on, you slob,' she said. 'Come to the park with me.'

Our dog, Prince, was already jumping up at the door with the lead in his mouth.

'OK,' I agreed with a sigh. I knew why Sonya wanted me to come. Sure enough, when we got to the park, my sister started asking questions.

Sonya was the only person who knew about my trouble with Meatball. She wanted me to tell a teacher. I shook my head.

'I can't *tell* on him.'

'I never heard anything so daft! Let me tell Mum and Dad — they'll sort it out. Or I could come and see this Meatball myself ...'

'No!' I shouted. 'That'd just make things worse ...'

Sonya thought this over. We had reached the field where you can let dogs off their leads. We watched Prince charging around.

At last Sonya said, 'Well, you can't go on like this. You'll have to sort it out yourself. I don't mean fight, but show them you're the kind of kid who won't be pushed around. It's all a matter of attitude.'

Suddenly, our dog raced up towards us, yelping. I saw why. A big dog was running after him. The dog only wanted to play, but Prince huddled behind my sister.

'That's Lucy,' said Sonya, pointing at the big dog. 'She's a big softy, but she scares Prince.'

Lucy was always round here, often without her owner. She lived in a house near the park, and she kept jumping over the garden fence and running here to play.

I looked at the big dog getting closer and closer with her tongue hanging out. *All a matter of attitude, eh?* I thought. *OK, let's see.* I stepped forward.

'Er ... shoo, please!'

Sonya saw what I was trying to do. 'Be firmer!' she said.

'Go away, doggie!'

Lucy thought it was a game.

YUCK!

She jumped up and began licking my face with her slobbery tongue.

'BAD DOG! SIT!'

A loud voice cut through the air. It was Sonya.

The dog dropped to a sitting position like a squaddie obeying a sergeant major.

'See?' said Sonya, slipping Prince's lead back on. 'You have to let them know you mean business. You've got to have the right attitude. The same goes for those bullies.'

Great, except for one thing ... What if you don't have the right attitude?

5

Being taught a lesson

Back at home, Mum said someone had telephoned – Neil Gregory!

'He seems like a very nice boy,' said Mum. (This was the highest praise Mum could offer.) 'Go and see him, dear. You need to start making some new friends.'

I shook my head. Neil wasn't the sort of friend I had in mind. But Mum went on.

'He said to tell you he's been working on something for dealing with meatballs. I didn't know you were interested in cooking.'

I froze. I knew only too well what the message meant – something to do with teaching Meatball Newton a lesson. My heart began to race with excitement.

I asked Mum for the address, and then I charged out and on to my bike.

Ten minutes later, I was at Neil's house. There was no answer, so I went round the back. 'Hello?' I shouted.

'In here!' a voice came from the shed.

Neil was sitting at a workbench. He had safety goggles on and he was soldering something. Some kind of machine was spread out in front of him.

The inside of the shed looked like an electrical repair shop, with TVs, radios, washing machines and fridges everywhere. Most had their backs off, so you could see all the working bits inside.

'What are all these for?' I asked.

'Spare parts.' He took his goggles off.

'I've been thinking,' he said, smiling menacingly.

He picked up the machine from the
workbench and strapped it on to his
back. A vacuum cleaner tube was
hooked to the machine. Neil held it like
a weapon.

'What is it?' I asked, totally puzzled.

'My anti-bully machine.'

He must have seen the disbelief on
my face.

'It wasn't so difficult,' he said. 'I *am* a genius, you know. Did I mention my IQ level? I should be in the *Guinness Book of Records*.'

Here we go again! I thought. The genius speech! But a part of myself, deep down inside, whispered, *Wouldn't it be great if he's telling the truth? What if this machine could teach those bullies a lesson?*

I remembered the other machine he had shown me. If Neil could build an anti-gravity machine, couldn't he build an anti-bully machine?

'How does it work?' I enquired.

Neil tapped the side of his nose and smiled.

6
Zapped!

KILKENNY
COUNTY
LIBRARY

You'd be surprised how few people bat
an eyelid when they see a kid walking
around town with a big, dangerous-
looking gizmo on his back. People
round here really mind their own
business, I suppose.

We wandered around for ages, and
only one grown-up asked us what we
were up to. Neil told him we were
testing his dad's new leaf-blowing
machine.

We walked for ages, but we couldn't find Meatball.

Then at last, we saw his two cronies, Adam and Phil, in the park. They had chased the little kids away. Now they were mucking about on the swings.

Neil marched up to them.

Neil's voice was cold. He spoke very slowly, as if he was talking to little children. 'We're here to teach you two bullies a lesson.'

Adam and Phil swapped glances as if to say, *Would you like to punch their lights out, or shall I?* They hopped off the swings, fists clenched.

Suddenly, I was feeling less confident about Neil and his amazing machine. 'Come on, Neil,' I said, nervously. 'Let's go.' I was almost ready to turn and run.

But Neil stayed put. His mouth was drawn in a tight smile.

As the bigger boys moved towards us, Neil gripped the end of the vacuum cleaner tube. His other hand clicked the *ON* switch.

The machine hummed. Then a jet of orange light burst out of the nozzle in Neil's hand. It looked like an energy field from some science fiction film.

Whatever it was, the two bullies were trapped in it. The air was filled with the fizz and crackle of the machine's beam.

But things got even weirder. I couldn't believe it!

Adam and Phil started to get smaller. They had both been taller than me, but not any more. Suddenly, they were shorter.

The tops of their heads would only just reach my chin. No, make that the middle of my chest!

They were getting smaller still! I watched them shrinking!

And here's the funny thing. In the middle of my shock and amazement, a part of me was pleased. *Let's see you push us around now*, thought a dark part of myself. Revenge really did feel sweet.

Adam and Phil's faces were frozen.

Did they know what was going on? I knew one thing – they were still shrinking! The two bullies only came up to my knees now!

They were wailing in fear. Their cries for help were so pathetic that I couldn't help feeling sorry for them. All at once I wanted this to end. It had gone too far. Suddenly, our revenge wasn't quite so sweet.

'That's enough, Neil!' I shouted above their cries.

But Neil's finger didn't move from the ON button. He just went on shrinking them more and more.

'Stop!' I bellowed at him.

Fear gripped me – no time to think. I had to do something and fast. I grabbed for the vacuum cleaner tube.

Neil swung around to face me. I had a split-second to see the look of shock and anger on his face. And then I was surrounded by a blinding orange light.

I heard Neil's voice saying, 'You're just like all the rest.' And that's when I fainted.

7

Racing against time

I don't know how long I was on the ground. But then I heard a tiny voice shouting, 'Get up!' I felt hands shaking me.

I opened my eyes and immediately wished I hadn't. I was still in the playground. There was no sign of Neil, but Adam and Phil were still with me.

Usually I would have felt a bit embarrassed about fainting. But that was the least of my troubles.

You see, I was as tiny as they were. We had all been shrunk!

Actually, I was probably the biggest of the three by a centimetre or two, but we were all about the size of Action Men. Or Barbie dolls!

The swings and slides loomed around us like the towers of a nightmare city.

Phil and Adam weren't acting so tough now. Their eyes shone with tears.

'Wh... what's going on?' cried Phil.

'That was Neil Gregory,' I said. 'He's a genius, if you haven't guessed already.'

'Wh... what are we going to do?' asked Phil, helplessly. 'I want to go home.'

I could understand why, but I knew we couldn't do that. I mean, what would we say?

Adam was just as scared as Phil. Somehow seeing my old enemies like that made me feel braver – more confident. One of us had to do something. It looked as if it was going to be me.

'No,' I said. 'There's only one person who can turn us back to the right size – Neil Gregory. We've got to find him. Come on!'

I began to run towards the canal.

If that's where Meatball was, that's where we'd find Neil.

Phil and Adam followed. We ran and ran. There was just one problem – when your legs are so short, you don't travel too quickly.

I soon had a stitch in my side, and we were still nowhere near the canal. It had started to drizzle. All our chances seemed to be washing away in the rain too.

''S no good,' I gasped. 'It'll take us forever.'

I was looking around for some way of getting a ride, when I heard an excited bark. I knew that bark. It filled me with terror.

It was Lucy, the big dog who was always in the park. She was bounding towards us. Adam and Phil let out little squeaks of fear.

'It's going to eat us!' Adam wailed.

I didn't think Lucy would eat us, but I was afraid of something almost as bad.

The big dog reached us and her tongue was hanging out at the ready.

This time when she licked me it was like having a bucket of water thrown over my head. Double YUCK!

I ordered myself not to panic and I yelled at the top of my tiny voice.

'STOP!'

And do you know what? She did! The dog stopped.

'Now sit!' I commanded. Lucy sat.

An idea hit me – it was crazy, but it might just work.

I climbed up on to Lucy's back. I took hold of her collar with both hands.

Phil and Adam stared as if I'd gone barmy.

'Quick! Sit behind me!' I ordered them.

I think they did it only because they were too stunned to argue.

When we were all sitting in a row on the dog's back, I told Lucy to run forward and she began to trot towards the canal.

It's a lucky thing that it was a wet and windy afternoon – the park was empty. That saved us from having to explain ourselves to any passing strangers.

On we ran. I used the collar to steer the dog.

Soon we were racing along the path by Thorny Wood. Not far to the canal now! We turned a corner.

In the distance, I saw two figures on the canal path, one tall and skinny, the other big and beefy. It had to be Neil and Meatball.

As we got closer, I saw Neil had his back to us. Meatball had put down his fishing rod and was facing him. Judging by Meatball's smirk, the bully had no idea what danger he was in.

I urged Lucy to go faster, but instead she slowed down. She wasn't daft. She knew something weird was going on, and she didn't want anything to do with it. Finally she just lay down.

There was no time to lose. I hopped off the dog and raced on ahead of Phil and Adam. I was close enough to hear Neil and the bully talking now.

Meatball said, 'I don't know what that thing is, but it won't do you any good.'

'That's where you're wrong, Meatball,' Neil giggled. 'You're always making people feel small. Well this machine is going to give you a taste of your own medicine.'

I panicked. What if Neil didn't stop shrinking Meatball? What if he just went on shrinking the big bully until he disappeared altogether? Until he was nothing? Even Meatball didn't deserve that.

I couldn't let it happen. I forced my tiny legs to go faster.

Suddenly Meatball spotted me. His smirk melted into a look of confusion, and then fear. He wasn't too bright, but even he knew something weird was going on when he saw a miniaturized kid racing towards him.

The muscles in my legs were aching, but I forced myself to go faster. Neil said, 'Bye, bye, Meatball.' His hand reached for the *ON* button. I put on a last burst – nearly there …

Click! The machine began to hum.

I jumped up into the air. My hand reached out for the button.

Whack!

The machine went silent.

I'd done it!

Panting, I stood between Neil and Meatball. Neil looked down at me, his face full of confusion.

'I don't understand. Why are you trying to protect him?' he asked me.

He meant Meatball, who was frozen with bewilderment. Neil went on. 'I only built the machine because I wanted you to be my friend, Steven. Don't you like me?'

He looked really sad. And that's when I understood. Behind all of his arrogance, Neil was just a lonely, awkward kid who wanted a friend. I could see him blinking back tears.

I knew the next words out of my mouth would be the most important I would ever utter.

I took a deep breath before I spoke.

'Course I like you ... but I can't help feeling a bit sorry for you.'

Neil's eyes speared me with their glare. 'Why?'

'Well, now I'm *sure* you must get nose bleeds up there!' I waited.

The smile started in Neil's eyes. Then he began to laugh out loud, and this time it sounded like a real laugh. I couldn't help myself – I joined in.

For the first time, we were like real friends. You know – more than just two kids who happened to have the same enemy.

'Now, if you don't mind, I'd quite like to be full size again. We all would ...'

Neil nodded slowly and gave me a shy smile. Then he turned a dial on the side of the machine. He pointed the nozzle back at me and at Phil and Adam.

This time the beam that shot out was blue. For a second, I saw only that dazzling, blue light. When it stopped, I was full size again. So were Meatball's mates.

'I was always going to change you all back, you know,' said Neil, shyly.

He opened a flap on the machine and pulled out a thin microchip. 'I don't suppose I'll be needing this any more. It's the brains of the whole machine,' he said. 'It's useless without it.'

He smiled again and then threw the chip into the canal.

It disappeared into the murky water with a soft *PLIP!*

'It needed more work, anyway,' Neil added.

I thought then that it was all over. But it wasn't.

I hadn't reckoned on Meatball. The bully's confidence was back. He had that look on his face – trouble on the way.

He jabbed a meaty finger at Neil.

'Useless, is it? Then maybe I need to teach *you* a lesson now, Beanpole.'

That's when I realized something.

I should have been afraid, but I wasn't. I had changed. Suddenly, Meatball wasn't so frightening to me.

I stepped in front of him. 'Pack it in, Meatball,' I said. 'There's been enough trouble for one day.'

There was a long moment's silence, then two more voices piped up.

Adam said, 'And me.'

'Yeah, come on. Call it a day, mate,' said Phil.

Meatball glared at us all. He didn't know what to do. First Neil's machine, and now his mates weren't backing him up.

Finally, he turned on his heel and stomped away.

8

An open secret

'And that was the last trouble we ever had from Meatball Newton. He never bullied us again.'

Chris looked puzzled. 'Why didn't I hear about all this before?' he asked.

'We all wanted to keep it a secret,' I explained. 'There would've been big trouble if it had ever got out. And, of course, Meatball wanted to guard his tough-guy reputation. He'd never tell.'

Chris nodded. 'But what about Neil? Did you two become friends after that?'

'Sort of. But once we no longer had a shared interest in getting even with Meatball and his mates, we didn't have much else in common. You know, I was interested in football and music, and he was more into radio astronomy and advanced physics.'

'So where is he now?' Chris asked.

I smiled. 'It was pretty clear that normal school wasn't enough for him. He knew more than all the teachers put together.

'In the end, he was sent to a special school, "The School for Exceptionally Gifted Children", something like that. It's a boarding school and he loves it there.

'In his last letter to me, he said he's working on a new invention.'

'What is it?' asked Chris.

'I don't know, but I bet we'll read about it in the papers!'

'Sounds likely,' said Chris.

We both took one last look at normal, old Thorny Wood School.

'You know, I bet it won't be so bad there,' said Chris.

We cycled off to enjoy our last week of freedom.

About the author

When I was growing up in Manchester, I always wanted to be an astronaut, a footballer, or (if those didn't work out for any reason) perhaps a rock star. So  it came as something of a shock when I became first a teacher and then an editor of educational books.

I have lived in Cambridge, Aylesbury, Oxford and Istanbul. I'm still on the run and live in America with my family.

I thought of this book because I wanted to write a story in which bullies get a taste of their own medicine.

Other Treetops books at this level include:
The Case of the Talking Trousers by Tessa Krailing
The Quest for the Golden See-Saw by Karen Wallace
Star Struck by Debbie White
The True Diary of Carly Ann Potter by Michaela Morgan
Cat Out of the Bag by Irene Yates

Also available in packs
Stage 13+ pack D   0 19 918702 9
Stage 13+ class pack D   0 19 918703 7